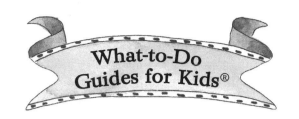

What-to-Do
Guides for Kids®

What to Do When the
NEWS
SCARES YOU

A Kid's Guide to
Understanding Current Events

by Jacqueline B. Toner, PhD

illustrated by Janet McDonnell

MAGINATION PRESS • WASHINGTON, DC
AMERICAN PSYCHOLOGICAL ASSOCIATION

Dedicated to free press and responsible, truthful, bias-free reporting—*JBT*

Books for Kids From the
American Psychological Association

Magination Press is a registered trademark of the American Psychological Association.
Order books here: maginationpress.org or 1-800-374-2721

Book design by Sandra Kimbell
Printed by Worzalla, Stevens Point, WI.

Library of Congress Cataloging-in-Publication Data

Names: Toner, Jacqueline B., author. | McDonnell, Janet, 1962- illustrator.

Title: What to do when the news scares you : a kid's guide to understanding current events /
by Jacqueline B. Toner, PhD ; illustrated by Janet McDonnell.
Description: Washington, DC : Magination Press, [2021] | Series: What-to-do guides for kids |
Summary: "The next book in our What to Do series about helping kids process scary events
and stories they are exposed to"–Provided by publisher.
Identifiers: LCCN 2020043597 | ISBN 9781433836978 (paperback)
Subjects: LCSH: Adjustment (Psychology) in children–Juvenile literature. | Anxiety in children–Juvenile literature. |
Current events–Psychological aspects–Juvenile literature. | Bad news–Psychological aspects–Juvenile literature. |
Mass media and children–Psychological aspects–Juvenile literature.
Classification: LCC BF723.A28 T66 2021 | DDC 155.4/1824--dc23
LC record available at https://lccn.loc.gov/2020043597

Manufactured in the United States of America
10 9 8 7 6 5 4 3 2 1

What-to-Do Guides for Kids®

**What to Do When
Bad Habits Take Hold**
A Kid's Guide to Overcoming
Nail Biting and More

What to Do When It's Not Fair
A Kid's Guide to Handling Envy and Jealousy

What to Do When Mistakes Make You Quake
A Kid's Guide to Accepting Imperfection

What to Do When You Dread Your Bed
A Kid's Guide to Overcoming Problems With Sleep

What to Do When You Feel Too Shy
A Kid's Guide to Building Social Confidence

What to Do When You Grumble Too Much
A Kid's Guide to Overcoming Negativity

What to Do When You Worry Too Much
A Kid's Guide to Overcoming Anxiety

What to Do When Your Brain Gets Stuck
A Kid's Guide to Overcoming OCD

What to Do When Your Temper Flares
A Kid's Guide to Overcoming Problems With Anger

What to Do When You Don't Want to Be Apart
A Kid's Guide to Overcoming Separation Anxiety

What to Do When Fear Interferes
A Kid's Guide to Overcoming Phobia

CONTENTS

Introduction to Parents and Caregivers

More than almost anything, we want the children we care for to feel safe. It's second nature to try to shield them from the harsher realities of life—but that doesn't always work. When tragic events happen, it's almost inevitable that children will learn about them. And sometimes life changes because of these events, and children need to know why.

Whether from television news reports, the car radio, or adult discussions, children are often bombarded with news. When the events being described include violence, extreme weather events, a disease outbreak, or discussions of more dispersed threats such as climate change, children may become frightened and overwhelmed. As a parent or caregiver, you may feel unprepared to help them understand and process the messages around them.

What to Do When the News Scares You provides a way to help children put scary events into perspective. If children start to worry or become anxious about things they've heard, there are ways to help them calm down and cope. Read through the book before you share it with your child to familiarize yourself with the ideas presented. This is not intended as a book for children who have themselves experienced trauma or loss; if you are looking for a book on that topic, I encourage you to explore Magination Press for other titles designed to help such youngsters.

Remember that children are impacted by the emotions of the important adults in their lives. Stay mindful of how your own reactions to frightening news events may influence the small ones around you. If the news is worrisome or threatening, you may feel a need to stay up to date on what is happening and to communicate with others about it. At such times, it may not be feasible to completely protect children from incoming information. But news reports and overheard conversations can lead kids to make incorrect assumptions of the danger to them or their family. Stories of individuals who are traumatized by an event may lead children to identify with those who are experiencing the event and make them think that they are next. When adults around them seem concerned, children's fears are unlikely to be whisked away by simple reassurance. They need help understanding what is happening and assistance in putting it into a larger context.

Keep these tips in mind as you help your child through scary times:

- Children's ability to cope with scary events varies with age and with the child.

- Limit young children's exposure to news stories as much as you can. When you are unable to limit their exposure due to your own needs for information, be available to interpret messages for them.

- Consider how you access news and how that may impact children nearby. Reading news on your own is the least likely to accidentally transfer information to children; television news is more likely to include frightening visuals and sound effects.

- Listen to the child's concerns before offering explanations. Ask what they have heard and what that information means to them. You may uncover misperceptions and unfounded fears which need correcting.

- Tell the truth but gently. Don't brush off a child's concerns but present hopeful information with the truth. Include information about how the event is being dealt with and people are being cared for. Be careful not to let your own fears result in sharing information based upon speculation about possible future developments.

- Help your child put the event in perspective. While you may have a sense that a threat is far away, limited in scope, being managed, or even in the past, don't assume that your child understands this.

- Comment to your child about the ways in which news reports may be making things seem more dire than they are.

- Help older children become active consumers of the news by teaching them which news sources can be trusted and why. Be sure to point out sources of information that are likely to be misleading, especially online.

- Remind the child that you and other adults around them will keep them safe. Use concrete examples when you can.

- Maintain routines and don't let news intrude on normal daily activities (no TV news during dinner).

Read *What to Do When the News Scares You* with your child to help them understand the news in context ("who, what, where, when, how") as a means of introducing a sense of perspective. This book helps children identify reporters' efforts to add excitement to the story, which may make threats seem more imminent, universal, and extreme. As you talk about scary events with your child, point out all the people in their life who keep them safe and some of the ways that they are doing so right now. If children become worried and anxious about events, encourage them to employ the coping

strategies presented in the book which are designed to reduce overexcitement and anxiety. Encourage them to develop plans of actions to offer support to others, participate in small ways to address large problems, and devise a family safety plan.

Scary news is an inevitable part of life. This book can support and guide you in your efforts to help scary news seem a bit more manageable for the young people in your care.

JACQUELINE B. TONER, PhD, is a clinical psychologist with over 30 years in private practice working with children and parents. She lives in Baltimore, Maryland.
Visit jacquelinetoner.net.

JANET McDONNELL is a writer and illustrator whose characters populate many books and magazines for children. She lives in Arlington Heights, Illinois. Visit janetmcdonnell.com, @McDonnellDoodle on Twitter, and @JanetMcDonnellIllo on Instagram.

CHAPTER ONE

Sometimes Scary Things Happen

Reporters let people know what is happening in the world. They tell news stories about things in your town, your state, your country, and also things that are very far away. There are a lot of ways that they let people know what they have found out. Some reporters write down what they have learned in a newspaper, magazine, or online. Others make reports on the radio or on TV.

Where do your parents usually find out what's happening?

_____

_____

_____

_____

_____

_____

_____

You may think that just knowing what happened is all that reporters do, but sometimes that's not enough information. Investigative reporters look further into things that happen to learn more about who the people involved are, what happened before, what might happen later, and whether anything like this ever happened before.

Sometimes the stories that reporters tell are scary. When bad things happen it's important that reporters let adults know about them. They might first hear about it from the news on TV, the radio, the internet, or a newspaper. Once some people hear about it, the news starts to spread. They start telling other people about it. They tell people near them and they call or text friends and family farther away to tell them what they've heard. Pretty soon lots of adults start watching the TV, listening to the radio, or looking for information on the internet and talking about what happened.

Lilly and Ben just finished dinner and their mom and dad turn on the TV news. The news person is standing in front of a big glass door and ambulances and flashing lights are all around her. Mom says, "Sorry kids, we can't play right now. Dad and I need to listen carefully." Then, Mom grabs her phone to call Grandma. Dad goes on the computer to look things up. They look very worried. Lilly and Ben feel worried too.

When something scary happens, pictures and information about it spread fast and it can seem as if it's all you hear about or see for a while. That can be a good thing because it can help people know if they need to do things to stay safe or to help others or know when the scary thing is over. But scary news can be upsetting and confusing too.

You may be reading this book because something scary just happened. Or, maybe one of your parents or a teacher knows that scary news is on your mind.

Draw a picture of something you saw on TV or heard about from the radio or another person that was scary.

Sometimes when you hear scary news you might not understand exactly what it means or how it might affect you. That can make it even more frightening. It's easy to get some wrong ideas about what the scary news might mean for you or people you know.

This book will teach you to **investigate** and figure out what is really happening. You might be surprised to find out that sometimes scary news isn't as scary as it sounds! But even when it's really scary, understanding exactly what is going on can help you feel less afraid.

When you investigate you may learn things that help you feel better. You might also find out that the scary thing isn't very likely to happen to you. And, you will learn some ways to feel calmer when scary news gets you upset.

CHAPTER TWO

What Is News?

News is just what it sounds like. It's something "new" that's happened. There are all kinds of news. There is:

Plain news:

There's a new street light in town.

Good news:

The weather will be warm and sunny today with a comfortable breeze.

Bad news:

The ice cream restaurant just closed.

And...there is **Scary news:**

There was a house fire in town.

When scary news happens, kids can have a lot of different feelings and may do things they don't usually do. When you hear scary news, you might feel scared but you might also feel:

sad

whiny

worried

Mad

grouchy

The important thing to remember about feelings is that it's okay to have them. Even feelings that are uncomfortable or make you unhappy are normal. The good thing about the kinds of feelings that you don't like is that they are temporary. They won't last forever.

It helps if you know what they are. Then you can talk about them or think about them more clearly, and you can come up with some ideas of things that can help you deal with them. You'll be reading more about this in a little bit (or you can skip to Chapters 8 and 9 if you want to learn a few strategies right now).

Sometimes after hearing scary news, you may do things you don't normally do.

You might

- feel like staying near your parents,

- start arguments,

- be mean to a friend or sibling,

- have nightmares,

- be afraid of being alone,

- be afraid of going to bed, or

- be afraid of the dark.

you might
BE
AFRAID

You might also have worries. You might worry that the bad thing could happen to you or your family or your friends. You might worry that a bad thing like that could take important people away from you.

If you start having worries it can help to talk to your parents, teacher, or other comfortable adults about how you feel.

Who are two adults who you can tell your worries to?

1. _____
2. _____

Devon hears a report on the TV news about a family that had a big house fire. The reporter says, "Unfortunately the Jones family lost everything." This sounds very scary. Devon is afraid that the same thing could happen to his family. He worries about what will happen to his house when he is at school tomorrow. Could his house catch on fire too?

Devon feels too upset to sleep. He tells his dad that he feels afraid and worried. His dad listens and understands how he feels. He tells Devon about things that he and Devon's mom do to keep the family and house safe. He reminds Devon of the fire drills his family has had and about the family emergency plan.

Devon still thinks a house fire sounds scary but talking to his dad has reminded him of ways his parents are protecting him, and that helps him feel safe.

Sharing feelings and worries can shrink scary ones down to size.

Write or draw about a time when talking to your parent or other grown up helped you feel less worried.

While it can sometimes be scary, it's important that reporters tell people (especially grown-ups) about all kinds of news. It's their job to help people know what's going on, even when it's upsetting.

19

CHAPTER THREE

Making the News Scarier

Reporters on TV, the radio, the internet, magazines, and newspapers want to tell a story that is **interesting.** To keep people interested they like to make what's happening sound exciting. That can be great when the news is about something happy, like a carnival coming to your town. They might talk about how the Ferris wheel is so high that you can see far away. Or they might show pictures of all the tasty treats that are for sale. Those details help people to imagine just how much fun they would have if they went there.

When it comes to scary news, though, making it exciting can also mean making it scarier. Just as with a report on a carnival, knowing more exciting details can make you feel like you are really there. But you certainly don't want to feel that way about a scary event! There are a lot of ways that reporters make news sound more exciting.

Sometimes when scary things happen, that news is repeated over and over again. It might seem like it's lasting longer than it is. Or it can seem as if the bad thing happened in lots of places even if it only happened in one place. It can even seem like something that happened yesterday is still happening.

Reporters may give examples of other times when similar bad things happened, and that can make it sound like these scary things happen a lot, even when this kind of scary thing is actually pretty unusual.

Watch a news show (it doesn't need to be one that's scary). **Circle** the ways in which they make things seem more exciting:

Loud, fast music

Focusing on exciting details

Quick changes of scenes

Including information about past events

Bright colors in the studio

Showing the same video over again

Talking fast

Talking loud

Showing different videos of the same thing over again

Talking about what might happen in the future

Interviewing people who are very upset or excited

Although she's never been near one, Olivia is really afraid of tornados. And now, the TV reporter is saying that there's one within 20 miles of her. She's not sure if that's close or far away or how far a tornado can travel.

Now the reporter is saying, "…and of course there was the tornado of 1902. It destroyed the town of Smallton completely. Farmer Jones' prize bull was lifted up into the funnel cloud." Does that mean the same thing could happen near Olivia's house?

What you see on TV or hear on the radio can be really confusing! It can be hard to understand what really happened. You may need the help of a grownup to make sure you understood what the reporter was saying. Sometimes **understanding** more about what happened can make it less scary.

When really bad stuff happens, people talk to each other about it. Sometimes rumors get started that aren't really true and can be even scarier than what did happen. Sometimes reporters talk about these rumors and this makes them sound true even if they aren't. You may hear them say that they've heard something that "hasn't been confirmed." This can be a clue that someone told the reporter a rumor but no one knows if it's true yet. If you hear something that worries you, check it out by asking an adult if it's true.

Ladies and gentleman, I just learned that we got a text from a viewer who says they saw another cloud that looked a bit like a tornado and it was very big. This has not yet been confirmed.

What would you show or say if you were a news reporter to make news about a kid falling off his bike sound more exciting?

Does this make it sound scarier too? _____

When reporters use techniques to make news sound more interesting, it can be confusing. All this added excitement can also give you some wrong ideas about what happened. Those wrong ideas can leave you feeling afraid or make you worry.

What's the Viewpoint?

TV can make you feel very involved in a story. For that reason, it is often the scariest place to get news because you not only hear about it, but you also see scary things. And like with all news, TV news shows do things to make it more exciting (and scarier).

Angel knew something was wrong when his mom rushed to turn the TV on in the afternoon. The news reporter said, "This appears to have been a random attack." As Angel watched the TV, he saw pictures of three people lying on the ground. The reporter talked to someone nearby and then there was a picture of three more people on the ground. Or... was it the same three people? Angel wasn't sure.

Then, another reporter said, "We are at Mercy Hospital where three victims have been admitted." Were they talking about the same people or three more people who were hurt? Angel felt confused and upset.

Sometimes the same thing is shown from **different angles.** This can make it seem like it happened more than once. A lot of times the news shows the same thing over and over again. It might seem like more people got hurt than really did when we see people falling down over and over again or when you see the same buildings being destroyed again and again.

TV reports may also use lots of **close ups** that make us feel like we're right there. That may mean that you see lots of upsetting details that you might not see even if you were standing nearby, because the cameras can zoom in closer than our eyes can see. Zooming in close can also make the places seem more crowded with people, too. This can make the scary event seem bigger than it really is.

Sometimes things that happen very far from where you live can seem very close. It might seem closer than it is because the place starts to seem familiar when we learn a lot about it and see lots of pictures of it. Sometimes it can feel like it's right down the street when really it's far away. It may be very hard to understand how close you are to what you are watching.

Explore a news report about a big event that isn't scary.

Where do you think it's happening?	
Do you think you could walk there?	
How long do you think it would take to get there by car or bus?	

Now, look the place up on a map.

Can you see how far away it really is?	
Can you figure out how long it would take to get there (you can ask an adult to help)?	

Are you surprised? ☐ yes ☐ no

The pictures on TV can also remind you of something you saw in a movie or TV show and you may get mixed up about what really happened and what was pretend. It can be helpful to check that out with a grown up.

Mom, that looks like the movie that we saw last week! The one where everyone was running from aliens from outer space!

Try watching a TV news report about something that isn't scary. Which of the techniques you just learned about can you identify?

Does the report:	Yes	No
Show something from more than one direction?	☐	☐
Does the reporter repeat things or ask other people questions so that they repeat what the reporter has just told you?	☐	☐
Does the reporter talk about similar things that happened at another time?	☐	☐
Is the camera zoomed in really close to the action or to the people talking?	☐	☐
Are there other things that could be confusing?	☐	☐
Do you know how close you are to the pictures being shown?	☐	☐
Does what you see remind you of a movie or TV show you've seen or a story you've heard?	☐	☐

When reporters do those kinds of things to make the news seem exciting, it can make a scary thing seem even more scary. Sometimes this makes kids feel upset and afraid.

Thinking carefully about the ways reporters make things exciting will help remind you to investigate more about what you're seeing and hearing.

CHAPTER FIVE

What's Your Source?

Reporters don't report everything they hear. When they learn about something that sounds important, they try to look for a lot of sources of information about it to make sure it's true.

Sources may be

- different people who witnessed what happened,

- people who were directly affected by the event,

- helpers,

- community leaders, and even

- books and news reports about past events.

They consider how **reliable** these sources are. People who are experts about similar events are more reliable because they are more likely to have accurate information about the event. Eye-witnesses are more likely to describe what happened than people who just heard about an event.

Julian is a reporter for his school newspaper. He is working on an article about ways to improve the sports program at his school. In order to be sure to understand the topic, he decides he needs different types of sources.

He talks to classmates to find out what kinds of sports they would like to add to the program.

The physical education teacher talks to him about equipment that could be needed for each sport.

The woman who owns the beauty shop in town tells him that local businesses would probably pitch in some money to help out.

Julian's pediatrician gives him a scientific article about how kids' fitness is improved when they participate in sports.

Look at a news report. How many sources did the reporter talk about? **List** the ones you can find and decide whether you think they are good sources, okay sources, or sources who may be giving incorrect information.

Source	Good	Okay	Misleading
_____	☐	☐	☐
_____	☐	☐	☐
_____	☐	☐	☐
_____	☐	☐	☐
_____	☐	☐	☐
_____	☐	☐	☐

A dangerous disease has broken out and is making many people sick. Pick up your reporter's notebook and get ready to interview some sources.

List three sources you think would provide the most important and accurate information about the illness and its possible effects:

sources

While you may hear news on the TV or Radio, many people also get news from the internet. If that news is from a trustworthy news agency that employs reporters, the sources they used have been checked to see if they are reliable.

But some information on the internet is not carefully researched. This can lead to incorrect information and false rumors being spread. Teachers and parents can help you look for clues to find out if what you see is likely to be true.

Mom, is this true?

Even trusted news organizations have reports that aren't based just on facts but are someone's **opinion**. Usually they provide clues to help you tell the difference between a news story and an opinion, but they can be easy to miss, especially when the news is scary.

Often people who are asked to give opinions are experts, but not always. If you hear an opinion that frightens you, ask an adult you trust about who the person giving that opinion is and whether they are believable.

Ask an adult to sit with you and look at a newspaper (it can be one that's online). Look for the words, **"opinion"** and **"editorial"** (that's a word for an article that is an opinion). Can you identify which articles are opinions even without reading them?

Now, develop a news website of your own. **Draw** a picture to show how you would help readers to quickly tell the difference between news stories and opinion articles:

Reporters do their best to choose truthful sources of facts to understand an event. This can include interviewing people who are likely to know about what happened, experts on similar events, and books or articles about past events or related scientific and historical information.

When someone shares their **opinion** in an article on a news site, it's important that viewers and readers are told that it is one person's **thoughts** and not a news report.

CHAPTER SIX

Keeping it Real

When you find out scary news, it can be confusing. Sometimes as you try to understand what has happened, you might have thoughts that worry you. Some of these thoughts can be **unrealistic.**

Unrealistic thoughts may be a little bit true but may also give you the idea that things are a lot worse than they really are. If something is scary, the last thing you want is to be extra scared about things that aren't even true! And sometimes those unrealistic thoughts can happen so fast that you might not even realize exactly what they are. This may be the time to do some investigative reporting of your own.

When reporters investigate a story, they try to get to the truth by finding the answers to the questions:

WHO? WHAT? WHEN? Where? HOW?

If you can answer those same questions you may find that you had some unrealistic ideas that were making an event seem scarier than it was.

Write a list of the adults in your life who you can trust to give you good answers to your questions about scary news.

_____

_____

_____

_____

_____

_____

Gracie was hearing a lot about climate change at school, from her friends, and from the TV. At first it made her want to do things to help the planet, like recycling and putting her lunch in reusable containers instead of sandwich bags.

But after a while she started worrying a lot about all the animals that would die, all the trees and plants that would disappear, and all the people who would starve.

She worried so much that it was hard to fall asleep at night. Gracie decided it was time to do a **Who? What? When? Where? How?** Investigation.

She asked her mom, **"Who** is going to be hurt by climate change and **who** can stop it?" Her mom told her that many people would be hurt but especially people in very poor countries or those who didn't have homes. She also learned that people, like her and her family, who were less affected might be most able to do things to help.

Gracie asked her dad, **"What** is climate change?" He explained that climate change was due to the earth warming just a tiny bit. That had led to changes in the weather and rising levels of seas.

Next, Gracie went to her teacher and asked, **"When** did climate change start and **when** will it stop?" Mr. Tappit told her that the pollution started way before Gracie was born and had gotten worse and worse. No one knew when it might slow down but now that scientists were learning more about it, people were trying all kinds of new ways to help.

Since Gracie's grandmother knew all kinds of things, she asked her, **"Where** is climate change happening?" Her grandmother told her that climate change was happening in big and small ways all over the world. She said some places had had terrible weather and other places had had droughts and floods. She said that their family was very fortunate that none of those very scary things had happened close to them.

Gracie knew that her neighbor, Ms. Scott, was a scientist. She decided to ask her, **"How** did climate change happen?" Ms. Scott told her that climate change was happening because people had been doing lots of things which created pollution in the atmosphere and only recently realized just how damaging that was.

how?

where?

when?

what?

who?

All this information was still scary but Gracie was less afraid and worried now. She understood that climate change was something that she and other people had to work on but she also knew that nothing really bad was likely to happen to her family, that climate change is happening over a long period of time, that it wasn't her fault, and that scientists are working hard to find new ways to slow it down. She decided she would try hard to learn ways that she could help.

Pick up your reporter's notebook and choose a news story (it doesn't need to be a scary one). What does it say about the event's:

Who? _____

What? _____

When? _____

Where? _____

How? _____

Information about a scary event is upsetting, and the way it's presented may lead to confusion. When you are confused you may also have some unrealistic ideas that make you worried. If that happens, try following the reporter's strategy.

Asking questions will help you to have a more realistic idea about the event and will prevent you from being frightened by things that aren't accurate.

CHAPTER SEVEN

What Is Un-news?

Un-news is stuff that happens all the time. It's not "new." It can be helpful to remember all the things that aren't news when you hear about scary news. Un-news is made up of all the regular things that happen all the time. It's not exciting. In fact, it can seem kind of boring. That doesn't mean it's not important though. In fact, paying attention to the regular things in your life that stay the same can help you to keep the news in **perspective.** That means keeping scary news in its place and not letting it seem like the only thing going on.

Here are some examples of un-news:

- kids went to school today

- the playground is open

- the supermarket has milk

- the traffic lights are working

- the wind was calm today

Can you **draw** a picture of some un-news that happened where you live today? What words would you use to explain your un-news?

Caption:_____

It's important to be able to notice un-news because the regular stuff that happens every day can help you remember the things that are safe and **"normal"** when you hear that scary things have happened. When news happens, a lot more un-news is happening in a lot more places.

There is big news in Manuel's neighborhood today. A kid fell out of a tree and broke his leg. Everyone is talking about it.

Manuel starts to think about all of the un-news that happened today:

- his mom cooked dinner,

- he played fetch with his dog,

- he did his homework,

- the girl next door rode by his house on her bike.

It sure seems like there was a lot more un-news than news in the neighborhood today!

Most of the time, un-news is actually more important to you. Usually, even when something bad happens, most or all of the normal things you do each day go on. And those everyday events and routines can remind you that you are safe. The next time you hear a scary news report, see if you can think about some of the un-news that happened to you and your family that day.

Put on an "un-news TV show" for your family. Can you make these events seem interesting? If you had the equipment, what kinds of graphics, music, or camera angles could you use to make your un-news exciting?

Un-news is made up of the regular, ordinary stuff that isn't really new at all. Un-news may not be exciting so it often gets overlooked, but when something scary happens, un-news can be comforting and remind you of how safe you are and that your life is still normal.

Taking Care of You

Your parents, teachers, and other adults will do many things to keep you safe and help you feel less upset by scary news.

Below is the beginning of a list of how adults take care of you. How many other ways can you think of?

* Police, firefighters, doctors, and nurses will respond to the bad event.

* Adults will listen to what you are worried about and answer your questions.

* Parents or others will do quiet things with you before bed to help you relax.

1. _____

_____

2. _____

_____

3. _____

_____

4. _____

_____

5. _____

_____

And, of course, there are things that you can do to make yourself feel better. Some are things you may do all the time, but if something scary happens, it's really important to keep doing them.

This includes things like:

- Eating healthy foods

- Keeping a regular schedule of sleep (and sleeping enough)

- Getting exercise

- Spending time with friends

? What are some things you do to take care of yourself everyday?

You can include ways you take care of your body and also things that help you to calm down or make you feel better when you are upset:

_____

_____

_____

_____

_____

It's important not to let scary news take over your whole day. That may mean not watching news on TV or the internet and not listening to it on the radio. Your parents may need to, but they will try to do it when you are not around.

Remember that if they say, "No TV right now" or "TV is just for grown-ups right now," they are not trying to keep you from knowing something you should know. They are trying to help you feel more comfortable.

It may be hard not to peek if your parents send you out of the room as they watch a scary news program. You can help them to help you feel more comfortable by finding something interesting to do to take your mind off of it. Or, you might need to do something to calm yourself down. Read on for some ideas of how to do just that.

Luca has been trying hard to take his mind off the news about an earthquake. He knows that it happened far away from where he lives. He also knows that it happened yesterday and is over now.

His grandfather explained that there were a lot of people helping those that got hurt. All of those things helped him feel better but Luca's body feels very wound up. He just can't seem to settle down.

When scary news makes you upset, you may feel it in your body. Even if your mind calms down, your body may still feel all the bad kind of excitement that scary news can bring. If you feel **wound up** and **upset** you might want to try some new ways of calming down.

One way of **calming down** is to do a breathing exercise. Here's one to try:

Sit comfortably on a chair or on the floor.

Close your eyes. Count slowly from one to five and use all the time that takes to breathe out all the air inside of you.

Then breathe in slowly, taking a count of five to fill up your lungs.

Do this three times. How slowly can you go?

When you're really worked up, it may be hard to concentrate on breathing slowly. If that's true for you, this next way of relaxing may be more fun. You can choose to sit but it may be more comfortable to lie down. Ask an adult to read the instructions to you the first few times you try it:

1. **Start at your toes.** Curl them as tightly as you can…tighter…tighter…even tighter! Now, let them relax.

2. **Next are your ankles.** Bend them hard so your toes point up to your knees…very hard… harder…hardest! Now let it go.

3. **Moving up to your legs,** squeeze your muscles tight…tighter…super tight! Now, ahhhhhh…let them relax.

4. **Now your bottom.** Make it really tense… squeeze…squeeze…SQUEEZE! Then let it become soft as a pillow.

5. **Now jump to your fingers.** Make a tight fist….tighter…even tighter…tighter still! Now let those fingers become weak and limp.

6. **Next, your arms...**squeeze...more...more... more...then let them flop like noodles.

7. **From here, go to your face.** Scrunch it up...your eyes, mouth, nose, forehead...scrunch and scrunch and **SCRUNCH!** Then ooooh....it feels so good to let it all go!

Sometimes it's important to do things that have nothing to do with the scary news, like:

- Doing something fun that can take your mind off of the news (like increasing the amount of un-news or even good news!)

- Spending time with your parents—reading together, playing a game, taking a walk

Write or draw about something you could do to take your mind off something scary in the news.

It's always important to take care of yourself, but when something frightening happens it is especially so. And when you're distracted by upsetting news, it's easy to forget to do the things that will keep you calm. You do many things every day that help you to stay happy and healthy. Keep doing those. If they don't seem like enough to keep you feeling calm, you now know some more things to try.

CHAPTER NINE

Making a Plan of Action

When something scary happens, it can make you feel very small and helpless. Taking some kind of action can help you to feel stronger. Scary news might start you worrying about something happening to you and your family. It can help to know how you and your family will stay safe.

Ask your parents if they have a family emergency plan. If they do, knowing about it can help you feel much better. If they don't, ask if they can help you make one.

When you talk to your parents about a family emergency plan, you might want to know:

? What have your parents done to keep emergencies from happening (like having a smoke detector or a house alarm)?

? What you are supposed to do if an emergency happens?

? Where would the family meet if you got separated?

Who besides your parents could help you and how would you reach them? For example, your parents might tell you to go to a neighbor's house and that neighbor might know how to get in touch with other relatives and friends who would come and help.

Work with your family to develop an **emergency plan.** Think about:

Where are all the exits of your house? If you needed to escape through a window, which ones are easily opened?

What should you say if you have to call 911? (Hints: you should know your address and be ready to say what kind of emergency it is).

Who is someone not in your immediate family that you can all contact if you get separated?

Does everyone in the family have other family members' phone numbers?

Where will you meet if you get separated?

What types of emergency drills will your family have?

When something bad happens suddenly, doing something to help other people can help you feel less afraid and give you a good feeling inside. You might:

- Write a letter or draw a picture to thank a police officer, firefighter, or doctor who is helping the people who had to deal with the scary event.

- Send well-wishes to people who got hurt and their families.

- Gather things together for a donation to help people affected by the scary event or bring things to help if something happens in your town.

Imagine that there is a big fire in your town. **Make a list** of things that you could collect from friends and neighbors to donate to people who lost their homes. Include things for adults and for children of different ages.

Items for Adults

_____

_____

_____

_____

_____

Items for Children

_____

_____

_____

_____

_____

Zawadi is feeling upset ever since she saw the news report about polar bears getting stranded when warmer seas cause the ice that they live on to break up. She worries about those bears and feels afraid for them. She wishes she could do something to help them, but she's so far away. And, after all, she's just a kid. Zawadi knows that seas getting warmer is tied to people wasting energy. She wonders if there is anything that she can do to change that…even a little.

Sometimes scary news can be about something that is ongoing, something that's happening gradually over time. Climate change and pollution are two of these huge, gradual, scary problems. It may seem as if you can't do anything to change things but keep in mind that small efforts by lots of people make for big change. You might:

- Think of ways that your family or school could reduce the amount of plastic used every day.

- Remember to conserve water by not letting the faucet run when you brush your teeth.

- Talk to your family about ways to reduce energy use in your home.

- Encourage friends to make the same changes that you have learned are helpful to the environment.

What is a big problem that worries you?

_____

_____

_____

What is a small thing that you can do to try to help make it better?

_____

_____

_____

Scary events can leave you feeling afraid and helpless. Finding ways to take action to make things better can remind you that you are strong and in control. You may not be able to change what happened or solve a big problem, but every contribution helps!

You Can Do It!

When bad things happen, it's okay to feel scared. But you now know that the news often makes events seem scarier than they really are. It can help to get a more realistic understanding of what happened if you do some investigation of your own. Using the kinds of questions that reporters ask can help. As you look into the **WHO? WHAT? WHEN? WHERE? HOW?** of what happened, you may find evidence

- that you and your family will be safe,

- that what happened wasn't exactly what it sounded like at first,

- that it's already over,

- that it wasn't as close as you thought it was, or

- that it wasn't anyone's fault.

In other words, as you investigate you may find evidence that you don't need to be quite as scared as you felt at first.

You've also learned the importance of paying attention to all the normal things that continue to happen at the same time as a bad event. As you do, you'll find that there are a lot more normal and even good things going on. That can feel calming.

But, if that's not calming enough, you now have some strategies you can use to calm your body down. And, you know that sometimes actions can help you feel better, too. The next time a scary story hits the news, you'll be ready to handle it.

YOU CAN DO IT!